T0288150

CITIZENS
OF
BEAUTY

POEMS OF
JEAN SÉNAC

TRANSLATED BY **JACK HIRSCHMAN**

CITIZENS
OF
BEAUTY

Michigan State University Press • East Lansing

♾ The paper used in this publication meets the minimum requirements
of ANSI/NISO Z39.48-1992 (R 1997) (Permanence of Paper).

Michigan State University Press
East Lansing, Michigan 48823-5245

Printed and bound in the United States of America.

22 21 20 19 18 17 16   1 2 3 4 5 6 7 8 9 10

LIBRARY OF CONGRESS CATALOGING-IN-PUBLICATION DATA
Sénac, Jean, 1926–1973.
[Poems. Selections. English]
Citizens of beauty : poems of Jean Sénac / translated by Jack Hirschman.
pages cm.—(African humanities and the arts)
Originally published under title: Citoyens de beauté.
ISBN 978-1-61186-199-0 (cloth : alk. paper)—ISBN 978-1-60917-485-9 (pdf)—
ISBN 978-1-62895-260-5 (epub)—ISBN 978-1-62896-260-4 (kindle)
I. Hirschman, Jack, 1933– translator. II. Title.
PQ3989.S468A2 2016
841.'914—dc23
2015017729

Book design by Charlie Sharp, Sharp Des!gns, Lansing, Michigan
Cover design by Shaun Allshouse, www.shaunallshouse.com
Cover artwork is an example of Pen Style Graffiti found in Algeria.

Michigan State University Press is a member of the Green Press Initiative and is
committed to developing and encouraging ecologically responsible publishing
practices. For more information about the Green Press Initiative and the use
of recycled paper in book publishing, please visit *www.greenpressinitiative.org.*

Visit Michigan State University Press at *www.msupress.org*

CONTENTS

INTRODUCTION

One of the most amazing phenomena in modern literature is that this book—first published in France in 1967, seven years before its author, an Algerian poet, was stabbed to death in his rat-infested basement flat—hasn't appeared translated in its entirety in the English-speaking world before now. Amazing, because this is a great work of human revolutionary affirmation.

I write this introduction on the Day of the Dead, the same day when, two years after Jean Sénac was murdered in 1973, another great poet, Pier Paolo Pasolini, was assassinated outside Rome. Both men were said to have been killed during or after homosexual encounters. In Pasolini's case Pino Pelosi confessed to the crime and served some six years in prison, only to declare, after his release, that he was not alone. He stated that a group of fascists had murdered Pasolini because of his writing—especially his "I Know" piece published in *Corriere della Sera*, the newspaper for which he wrote a column in which he announced in a poetic exposé that he knew who was behind the corruptions in Italy, and he prophesied the economic and political *tangentopoli* in Italy fifteen years later—and because of his movie *Salò*, which is perhaps the most courageous movie of the twentieth century, revealing the relationship between sexuality and fascism.

I'm not taking a detour from my journey here with Jean Sénac. As Pasolini's other killers were never brought to justice, Sénac's killer or killers have never been identified, leading many to believe that his death was by fascist or fundamentalist hands.

Like Pasolini, Sénac was an extraordinary poet. Born in Algeria in 1926 to a Spanish woman, Jeanne Comma, Jean was the bastard son of a supposed rapist. He knew nothing of his father, and he took the name of a Frenchman, Edmund Sénac, who was married to his mother for a short time.

Between 1954 and 1961, the time of the Algerian war for independence, Sénac was in self-imposed exile in France, but he always spoke of himself as an Algerian. Because he had been a *pied-noir* (a settler in Algeria who spoke French) yet had ties to FLN (the National Liberation Front), which was fighting to overthrow French colonial rule, his life was always tensed between his European descent, through his mother, and his North African dream of liberation for Algeria.

In France, Sénac's poetry was influenced by René Char, and his need for a father figure was answered by another Algerian, Albert Camus. Camus and Sénac's relationship was close for some time, even intimate, but Camus wanted Algeria to retain its French influence, and he condemned Sénac's great socialist poem "Salute to Black Writers and Artists"—revealing something about the myopia of the famous novelist. Sénac was in fact an advanced revolutionary for the Algerian people in the sense that he'd been schooled in the class struggle of Marxism and Leninism.

In 1962 Sénac returned to Algeria where, in addition to supporting the Ahmed Ben Bella government, he was a founding member and Secretary General of the Union of Algerian Writers. He hosted a popular radio program for almost a decade, featuring the poetry of Walt Whitman, Nâzim Hikmet, Federico García Lorca, Bob Kaufman, Allen Ginsberg, and Luis Cernuda, as well as Arab-speaking poets (though Sénac did not speak Arabic) and other poets who sent their works to him.

With the poem, "Citizens of Beauty," written after a visit by Che Guevara to Algeria, Sénac fused his dreams of socialism with sexual, particularly gay, desire, which set off his eventual estrangement from the Union of Algerian Writers.

By 1965 a military dictatorship had ousted the socialist leader Ahmed Ben Bella, whom Sénac adored and worked for. Always confronting injustice and oppressive ideological turns, Sénac went so far as to publish an anthology of new Algerian poets written in French in 1971, playing the *gaouri*, a foreigner or infidel, to the end of his life. Like all true communists and socialists, he welcomed all the languages of the human pantheon, including the Arab-language poets. Ironically it's been suggested that Jean was one of the first poets martyred by fundamentalism.

∎ ∎ ∎

When I came to San Francisco in late 1972, the City Lights Book publishing company was at the corner of Grant Avenue and Filbert Street. I had edited and translated some of the *Artaud Anthology* for City Lights, and I found a typescript of a poem entitled "Le Mythe du Sperme-Méditerranée," by Jean Sénac, in a basket on a desk at the publisher's office. I made a photocopy of some ten pages of the manuscript, and my translation of that material was published by the young North Beach poet Irwin Irwin a few years later as *The Myth of Mediterranean Sperm*.

I knew nothing about Sénac at the time, but I found that he had published a book, *Citoyens de beauté*. I was curious and sent for it, and in 1974 I translated it while living on the Alleghany Star Route near San Juan in the Sierra Nevada Mountains.

I sent the translation to five different publishers in the '70s and '80s, but none of them wanted to publish it. In the '80s the late poet David Moe rented a number of plastic news-boxes and, using lurid and semipornographic covers, distributed a newspaper of world poetry, *Lovelights*, which published more revolutionary poetry and translations than any journal or magazine in the United States for almost a decade, including one of my translations of Sénac's work.

This book's power resonates with the camaraderie that one finds in Walt Whitman's "Song of the Open Road," one of the greatest poems written in the American language and one which surely influenced the Algerian poet. His tribute to Whitman is an obvious reference, but Jean's very open, politically erotic, and collectivizing metaphors throughout the book engage the imagination wholeheartedly, whether masculine or feminine.

In 2014 *Ambush Review* in North Beach, edited by Bob Booker, printed the first section of Sénac's poem to Whitman. My thanks to him and to Kenneth Harrow, who understood the significance of Sénac's work and began the process that brings you the work of this most neglected and important poet.

—*Jack Hirschman*

CITIZENS
OF
BEAUTY

Citizens of Beauty

For Ahmed Hounaci

And now we'll sing love
for there's no Revolution without love,
no morning without smiling.
Beauty on our lips is one continuous fruit:
it has the precise taste of sea urchins one gathers at dawn
and relishes when the Golden Sea Urchin breaks away from the
   mists and warbles its song on the waves.
Because everything's song—except death!
I love you!
Revolution, you've got to sing the endless body renewed by Woman,
the hand of a Lover,
the graceful curve, like a writing on space,
of all those passersby and all those travelers
who give our march its genuine light,
our heart its impulse.
O all of you who establish serene or violent beauty,
pure bodies in the tireless alchemy of Revolution,
incorruptible gazes, kisses, desires in the groping of our struggle,
points of support, real points punctuating our hope,
O you brothers and sisters, citizens of beauty, come into the Poem!

• 3

Here's the sea. The bay (because it's a fruit of light and our gaze).
Young bodies are full of traces from the sea.
(I repeat myself because beauty is infinite recognition on our page
   ...)
All is light and sings while Revolution fashions its instruments.
Here's the sea. Your body, salt marsh where, thirsty, I hold sway.
Let's drink the sea. I'll drink your soul.
Salt-drunk. Thirst-drunk. In little gulps I drink your soul.
What space in our most sealed-off connections!
What mutations in that plundered still!

You radiate, a carrier of planets,
from the depths of abysms of linen.
Over the other slope of ourselves
we're seesawing. Here's the sea.

Here, the fields. The vine-shoots scowl. But the buds, the trimmed
        grass, the earth
big as your hips! And palms the length
of wide tarred roads. Let's sing love
for Revolution on this earth is the component of essential fertility.
What glory in the simple look of an infant under that veil!
What promise! May the afternoons here be disrupted,
perpetually new in their modulations
—Who can sing the same song twice here?
And now love has no more power to speak.
New grenades are bursting in our teeth,
the pomegranates of popular conscience, the fruits!

Your body was almost impalpable, and I all but read through it with
        my lips,
so immense was the multitude of sunlight upon you
and the sand around.
(The words—tell me, O my love, the words we're going to make over,
make them spick-and-span so they're no longer ashamed in the vein
        in the stone where misfortune's put them,
so they can cut loose, winging through the streets, onto the Pier, into
        fields
like you, so that they wear a smile becalmed. In
the mouth of words, the density of the sea, the density of your lips!)

Beauty on your lips is one continuous flame,
the bird of sunlight who's bent on its miraculous laying of eggs
—and succeeds!
O I'm never done greeting the day, putting my delight
in daily order, arranging it on your body,
giving life to the alphabet of the dream!
I love you. The Revolution rises
through the sheer symphony of young bodies fronting the sea.

And we're brought near. What a marvel, faithful earth,
What goodness!
Beauty was there, for the firstcomer, in the opening of his hand,
vulnerable and wild, a fruit balanced
between gaze and hunger. In me
many birds, many birds
fluttering, the words are putting on
marching sandals. Revolution,
what an afternoon it was!
I've seen the most beautiful people on earth
smiling at the fruit and the fruit giving itself.

For the fruit, should you invite it to the banquets of men,
will rush up.
Exploding like a pupil.
You think he's chaotic, he swims with ordered strokes.
Listen to the urchin, the medusa
who unfolds in order to defend itself:
a melody of space—and the cosmonaut responds.
Your heart doesn't burst with joy; it's rounded-off, composed.
Peace is sweet on our skin.

I love you. You're strong as a government committee
                    A farm cooperative
                    A nationalized saloon
          The afternoon rose
                    The unity of the people
          A literacy cell
                    A professional center
          A word from meddah
The fragrance of jasmine in the rue de Tayeb
          A gouache by Benanteur
The song of walls and the metamorphoses of slogans
                    The soleá of my mother
                              The blues, the browns of Zerati
The swimmers at Pointe Pescade
                    The Timgad Black
                    The Venus of Cherchell
                    My heart, my graffiti.
I love you. You're my positive lunacy.
                    Like a very red watermelon
          The smile of Ahmed
          A Chinese kimono
                    A djebbah of Jasmina
     A beautiful political discussion
          A wagon full of laughs
     A girl taking off her veil
               Another putting it on
          A butcher posting a sale
               A successful performance
                    The applauding crowd
          Jean who lays another
          On a rock and names the land
     The spurt of water in the yard

As on the night of bouqala
A priest from Djelal
An elegy by Anna Greki
A mathematical formula
The history of Medjnoun
And his Leila
The procession of November 1st
The certainty of Bachir
The steps of Odessa
The olives of Tilioua
A dancer of the hadaoui
El Anka and his dove
Yahia who peels the noun
Natalie who spells

One Orange.
You're my action poetry. I love you.
Yes, you're strong, you're beautiful
like words that find their place
on the sheet.
Our healed sorrow,
Our miracle of pardon,
like the walkways on terraces,
The satellite that answers
like a pebble between your hand
and mine,
bearing witness to summer.
Together we've confronted ridicule,
acquired habits, the current images,
the steelworks of capital.
The harvests were good this summer.
The sea true blue. Almost green. I love you.

And now for our kids I speak the color of Tolga,
that blue that's come rapping at the window,
not a sea-blue but a deeper bed
for the simple leisure of the soul.
And our heart so like a bedsheet, in that blue we've crossed
(look, it's burning!),
the blue smile of Tolga among its ruins and palms!
And the dignity of El Hamel!
M'Chouneche, which crackles with audacity at the bottom of gorges!
I'll never be done rousing our ironworks,
I'll never be finished naming the infinite
prolegomena on your body . . .

                            O patient and headstrong
Revolution!
                    O those teeth that are the white page
where my poem is constructed!
                       O mellowest night
in the absinthes of your arms!
Yes, don't be afraid, tell them
that you're beautiful like a government committee
                    A farm cooperative
                    Like a nationalized mine
O my love, let's risk dressing the body
of the new poem in new flowers!

And even if the horror confronts us now
(for nothing's easy, no, everything's in endless suspense).
If our bloated monkeys on café terraces
nibble at the future along with the peanuts
and speak of Ben M'Hidi as of an object of harmless consumption
(O brother-dynamite! O naked brother-flame!

O active brother-wind who roots out the gangrene!),
even if discouragement and derision attack us,
we know now that we're saved
in the great socialist motion
for Revolution and Love have renewed our flesh
(Salut! Salut, tzaghrit and grains, a hundred times over!)
I love you. Near the sea
the children of the alphabet are rising in joy like reeds.
We sit ourselves down in the shadow,
and you're astonished
because an animal for god's sake has come and plopped itself down
        on my knee.
Yes, those who've perished have not deceived us.
That's why we're singing love now.   • 9

Algiers, January 1963
Pointe Pescade, October 1963

Arbatache

For Kayasse

1.

This evening you draw near me more confident than usual.
You've planted your tree.
Its stock's replanted along the walkways in sweat,
in smiles.
Yesterday's tensions no longer make sense,
nor do those tensions we tear out of ourselves
one by one.
Let's speak of Arbatache the way one speaks of
Soummam or the Sierra Maestra,
the way one speaks of Odessa or the Paris Commune,
the way one says, You're beautiful, You're grown-up, You can read.
Our flag is green: the crowd that replants
and the heart that bounds toward the sea in August.
So many nights have passed and so much night gnaws at us:
it was the land that screwed the party.
Today you repeat: "Look, Yahia, we've held back the land, we've kept
      life back."
Where's the poem now
save in the hand that rises to affirm our harvest,
save on our lips where the tree's
already fruited and the bird's
brought a bit of the sky back?
I'm dreaming, we're dreaming
                    to the rhythm of passing trucks.
And I hug you, my child,
more confident this evening for having planted your tree.

Then he sinks into the opacity.
My shadow's rotten, he thinks.
I'm a tree all scarred,
a mess of nerves where birds get drunk
and fall into the mud tearing their feathers.
It was an autumn nightmare.
The untouched mob around him constructed a dam
against death.
Am I a traveler from another world?
A residue of many mistakes?
Once again the Child leaps up onto its heart:

I've planted my tree!

3.

He knew that Revolution
makes a brick of a smear,
a quarry stone of a cinder.

He knew that night is short
despite long, long hours
for him who puts a sun in the corners of the house.

He knew that the Child's trust
is more fertile than our dramas
and dominates our lack of good sense.

He knew that our flesh

decked out to be corrupted
is quick to recoup its brilliance.

One day our mountains will turn green again.

4.

But on this arid day, happiness itself
is crossing our body and not stopping.
The sea can come pounding, and our vertebrae
will open to an infinite overflow,
all around there being only weariness and disorder.
To be asked even if friendship, love sprouting over this land,
hungry only for bread, justice and an impetuous enjoyment like
        oblivion.
The jaunty enemy—uncalled-for!—has battered us for so long
and the vineyard has clutched its shards to this heart
so that there's no longer place for a welcome word
or a flower in a window.
Look at those mountains: not a single rose!
No woman's hand for a rose!
Only worldly emaciation and barking dogs!

5.

A tree and some bread, that's what they're asking for,
and a little fun in town,
a little night-towning: alcohol, the twist after the war!
And a little female saliva on wounds that are still raw.

But where's the rose? Where's the tree, the bread?
The gilded word that isn't a politesse, a frill?
Where's respect? Honor?
A chill from way up north is passing over this land.

6.

But the tree comes on. Always, even if you remain aloof, it comes on.
It shakes your sick old body and aims its bird at the sky.
Between vineyard and charnel house, it mumbles a word
that leads the sun to your lips, and you're singing!
Arbatache, because the people are on the rise!
Arbatache, because your shadow is possible,
even holey, even black!
Arbatache, because our very tears
are going to irrigate the soil
so fleeced, so smutted!
Arbatache, because life is stronger
in the tiny fist of a Child
than in a bureaucrat's hand!
Arbatache, because you'll stumble 40 times
on the road and still scrape together your tools!
Arbatache, because at the end of the sadness
there'll be a planted tree!
And tomorrow, the Rose!

7.

The earth is crumbly, welcoming, but your soul's a rock
of solitude.

The tzagrit of women, the hands
of kids on your chest
are only passing cart tracks.
Nightingales of exile.
It's because night has built its bridges in splendor,
and because the darkness is rich,
and you watch over that gritty treasure with pride. How many
        centuries
are scattered in your bones?
What torrents swirl in you, carrying the taste of the dead
to your heart? For it is death
that's taken you by the waist and is dancing, and you know it.
Come back! Come back to us! Hold on to the land!
Hold on to what's left of clarity in you!

8.

Yé mmâ! Yé! Like a well
stuffed with rotten barley, I resound.
At the rim, barely a drop of rain.
And the sun, the sea? That was yesterday. Yé mmâ!
I hook myself to a blade of grass, to a smile, to the sound
—Roots!—to any sign more violent
than this nightmare where I'm biting
the earth!
Yé mmâ, the earth my accomplice
and not a eulogy to happiness!
There's got to be time for the pickaxe
to arrive at the heart, to split the marble
and for the grain to blossom.
(You know it, my farm boy!)

The sun that drives everyone nuts is now and not forever!
Look, I'm calling for you like a child that's erupti . . .
Yé mmaaaaaaaaaaaaaaaaaaaaaaâ!

9.

A hugged body is never a dam
against the night but contrariwise
is a shift of restlessness that burns
till dawn and recalls you to the center
of sorrows. If you build
a citadel of muscles
the worm will get to you and you'll stagger
drunk with your corruption.
But sometimes the earth opens outward.
You plunge in, swim
toward the root, you struggle
surrounded by mirrors, you reach
a clear space vaster than the sea.
It's there the trees that you haven't planted,
the burst-open fruits, and the smell of the ancient
darkness are waiting for you. You bite into the fruit
faithful to your obstinacy. What mocking
fidelity! Death
resumes its dance on every hugged body.

(What root have you been looking for for 16 years,
or what splinter to take out of your body?)

10.

If you bite into earth, you can
always keep its taste nestled in a tooth.
You've wanted to cry out: They're all rotten!
Lemme hear Rameau, El Anka, Djamila,
lemme hear my mother—her naggings in poor taste,
lemme lose myself in these drawings the kids are scribbling with
       chalk on the Pointe Pescade streets,
lemme, lemme—deck out your boats,
fatten you up at the bashes!
What do your brawls and your works mean
when my people are dying of hunger?
O young ones! O high schoolers, fellahin, jobless ones of the towns
       and starving ones of the douars,
get yourselves up and raise up your alphabets, your oral culture
       against their mediocre verse!
Those worms are already gnawing at our roots.
But the root is stronger than their nibblings.
So, on with the feast.
Bite into the earth and keep its flavor in a tooth.
A tooth for the poor, a head-strong, furious and fine
tooth for loving and a healthy hunger.

11.

. . . .
. . . .*

---

* To appear

12.

"My people are alienated, tortured, de-brained;
my people are suffering, and there's no bread."*
No, brother, it's not the colonist monsters any more,
it's the napalm of our own bourgeoisie, of profiteers, of "militants"
            without foundation
—and it's not a dead hand they're putting out!
The enemy hasn't changed for them:
it's the patriot, the people.
They're sabotaging everything so that nothing moves.
Masked behind high-bids, ass-licking, and diplomas,
they infest the streets of our towns and the offices; leprosy's fallen on
            our douars.
Comrades, the shits are invading our blood!
There's corruption and crime.
Militant-agents, brothers at bottom, brother president, look at them
            slobbering:
the blood of Ben M'Hidi is their Coca-Cola.
Those who are learning are the people;
their place is with us.
Those who've taught nothing are the executioners of the people.
And the executioners are strutting through the streets this evening.
So?

---

* Extract of a poem, "Morning of My People," written in July 1956 and published in this epoch in
the review *Esprit*.

13.

Let's get going, leave all that bitterness behind.
Write and carry the best of your rhythm to the people
—not the falterings, not the jealous rat race,
but the Impulse, it alone (which lifts off to the heights).
The Revolution's giving you the high sign, the smile of Ben M'Hidi
and up there it's all simple: on a level with your arms.
I've had a really awful winter, have seen the best copping out to the
        mediocre—and braying!
I've pasted some tenacious butterflies up on the night.
My head's hummed from airplanes from Paris and those from
        Havana:
to escape, escape, never for an instant forgetting the people!
"Be well," repeated Mohammed, who organized self-management.
and "Thanks," Kayasse added.
Thanks for what? Thanks to me?
To you!
I'm a fist of landless grains in springtime,
a handful of useless grain
confronting the great schism of my voice.
I was taking refuge in my sheets—the laments of the sea lacerating
        me to the bone.
Where are we headed in this ferocious exile?
And you, Revolution, what tooth are you hidden in?
I interrogate the night, the crowd,
the smile of Ali, of Abderrahmane,
the one of Lumumba full of spittle, Yveton, Thuveny, mutants of a
        crazy hope;
I ask Khemati: Brother, help me one more time,
I telephone Amar, Bachir, Robert, Mourad, Jean, Djamal;
I rediscover my walls, stressed out, lucid.

But where's the sunlight been shipped to this time?
Where's my Republic of the Poor?

14.

You come back. You've planted your tree.
You smile. Your smile has retained the land.
Child,
wash me clean of death,
wash me clean of the mud.
I'll put my verses on your lips and if they rise
I'll leap so that my days no longer are an exile.
For a stem already is starting up from under my words.
A stem! And tomorrow, the Rose! The Garden! The Forest!
We're alone, but we're in solidarity.
But are we alone?
Withhold the earth, Child, withhold the earth in my heart.
Slogans no longer are enough,
—they don't suffice, but sing,
sing to be done with power and you'll fill our body with the
        conspicuity of forests!—
A hard, daily patience is what's needed
—the cedar, the carob tree—
and higher than disheartenment
—the oak, the eucalyptus, the olive—
the power of believing in the fruit despite the dead branches
—the palm, the pine, the orange-tree, the aloes, and the mimosas—
the dead men, if only they were! But no, they're vicious, arrogant,
        aggressive.
You have to plant a tree—another one, your own tree
—one for every slain brother, for every sister.

This is the long march, my child—and our ankles are bitten.
Socialism's a long road, and the brigands are constantly whetting
        their irony and barbed wires.
But there's your smile, and there's the Tree—the Bétoumier tree!
You have to fight, march on, struggle to recapture the sense of '54.
To fight and lay seed. Plant and protect the plant.
And defend the Tree. Find out the meaning of '64.
The patience and working-class certainty.
The joy of keeping on keeping on. The song.
Let's get those marching sandals on.
Let's advance toward Love.
Let's advance toward the Rose!

Pointe Pescade, December 1–24, 1963

The Night of Doubt

For Mireille and Jean de Maisonseul
For Reski Zérarti

I.

DIRGE FOR A GAOURI

1.

Don't ask the poet for his autograph, punks.
It's been a long time since I used a pen rather than my mouth!
My sun? It's the hedgehog in the slime I've pulled all the bristles
   from one by one.
I got no other signature but a lusty kiss.
Words bleed in my
     fingers.
I go forward, wide-open-
handed.
I don't write any more, my hands are too full of things to see.
Once upon a body I was an aviary,
       and the poem
went from one group to another,
a carrier of bread, anise, and fresh onions—the party
packed the terraces. Listen:
the Bartók elegy, when day and the end
of things encounter each other, is developing. We wanted wine.
I wore my death sandals.
Flowers
stuck out their beaks, the waves their teeth,
but nothing could hold back the greedy pilgrim. He bites
in order to go forward. He dies
in the odor of his words. He wears
the wrinkle of dread on his face. A pall
is pulled over his scruff where sunlight once . . .

2.

"Don't ask the poet for his autograph, punks.
Your signature is more spacious,
a slowly burning mischief bent on the only space that concerns us:
where the future whirls
in all letters and dawn is on your teeth!
Smile on the sands while the sea comes over us,
sweep away the rubbish, storm the iron grating.
I won't hold a pen in my hand,
I want it free to sketch our joy,
available for uniting with yours.
The afternoon's approaching . . ."

                                        That's what I was writing
barely a year ago.

3.

Don't ask for anything, punks, but just smile
for the poet. It's the last sliver holding his body
at the cliff edge. The sea
was an expanse of joy, the
opacity engulfing what remains of soul in me. I'm
a whirlwind of negations and disorder. I write
a poem on your eyeballs with my nails,
punks . . . The End.

4.

I only know how to sign with a lusty gaze
on the sands while
your muscles are stretching: life!
And my flesh goes crazy . . .
Ideas don't come from barricades.
They moan under my skin. Teenagers
in the stadium trample on the verb, and grass
invades our blood. Was that the glory?
That was poetry? O
what a mockery!

5.

I deny what's only the darkness in me.
My bones are becoming
liquid and flowing toward
the sea. The sea!

6.

A jangle of rhythms invades my memory and
tangles up the roots. Where's
my heart? I'm nothing
but a cart of bells. I've only
got a pack of wasps in the spot where
voice once sang.
I've no more jump, conscience, than I have orgasm. Where
am I? In what

waking state? Rushing
toward what other misery?
Death is the limpid hook-up. O
sentences, pull a cry up out
of my dream again!

7.

So that kids can testify I wasn't just a can
of shit.

8.

But
beat on down
again
you
sunlight!
Vigor
on
my living
         bones again,
beat on down!

9.

And don't stop grabbing for that tenderness on my lips that you
        might possess one day.

Nothingness. But if . . .
No, only waste
while the body liquefies
dizzily toward the tide.
Fish, nets, boats, shoreline—it's an imagery
to stay alive by
one more season. But my soul's
got no jump anymore. Arrogant,
it needs a South African death.

11

I question.
I straighten up on my bench and call out.
No autographs, punks, but a place among you
for believing there'll still come a day
more resolute than exile.

For it's this exile,
endlessly, the refused
place. Can one live
without a homeland. Without the
more intact SA homeland. The body
is torn, faded
(old blue jeans with tears).
When the land is refused him,

which was
even with its brambles,
rubble, and corrosions
of blood his very own!
(Land, which is the motionless form of a people,
its most secret density, architecture and panoply.)
I'm destroying myself like one
who loves without an answer. The sea
is nothing but a very harsh coolness
where my days knock together . . . I was
naked in the verb. I'm
a raven in rags
reeling toward the abyss with a

who-cares if this land isn't mine!

13.

I wasn't born for these laments or so that
the rose shatters at my song. I've carried the splendor
of daylight on my fist—nubile falcon of my dreams.
Let the hunts be—uplifting phrases! What drunkard
starlings on our lips! What nights
with the nightingale like a sun of ashes!
Living had that dry taste of fish eaten
under the arches of El Djezair, and the savor of sauces—
—laurel, cumin, garlic, and a spot of shadow
where the concoction simmers.
I love you, but what for? I'm talking in a void!
I've abandoned my love to the grasshoppers of Europe.
Revolution! I've given all, and for what?
A rolling dune

and not a chimera where this face can rest!
Each day one desire, then two or three through the door.
I've run after bodies—O hay-harvesters! Shanties!
Dawn is crumbling with the sea.

14.

Punks, don't ask a gaouri poet, not him, for his autograph.
What calligraphy is there outside of goodbye!
O don't mix him up with your numbers, which are about flares,
        terraces, harvests.
For how can he, if a stranger in his land, carry his people's hope with
        him?
How can he, as one refused his land, find a walkway for his
        footsteps?
For it's there one gets down to the roots.
And it's there that I say: let's replant together,
and it's just there that the pack rises up,
yelping not for construction
but to put the blood
                up for sale, rather than
to dry it.
The pack knows only how to smile,
but look at its teeth!

15.

gaouri
        goat
gaouri

                              goat
              gaouri
                              goat
              youpin
                              little rat
              roumi
                              melon
              goat
                              gaouri
              goat
                              gaouri
              goat
                              gaouri

If the new man doesn't invent a vocabulary that's the measure of his
        consciousness,
may the new man crumble.
If the new man's consciousness remains a gambling house where
        vices go hand in hand,
may the new man perish.
If socialism is an emollient salve under which the wounds remain,
may socialism shatter to bits.
If the new man doesn't invent a new tongue,
if he attends to misfortune with constant misery,
may he and his language and his newness die,
may the fire ravage them!
From the essence, comrades, from the essence.
So long,
        Brothers.

And we would have been able to love one another . . .

16.

O that song lying in wait for me
for centuries.
The misery of the old, the sorrow
of adolescents at the gates of Grenada
(the lament of Boabdil goes up in flames on their lips!)
and in the rubble of Elche, that miner who offered up his guts for the
        epoch.
(Time's faked us out a consciousness and an ear
—bad faith, doubtful memory:
the times have gimmicked up our blood!)

17.

When I die, punks,
take my body to the sea.
Listen to the siguiriyas—the Irretrievable, where my Arab ancestor
        weeps,
listen to El Anka: "Ya dif Allah,"
and the orchestra concerto of Bartók.
I've hungered for beauty for 37 years through such things!
        I've hungered for a state of health!
Be patient. It's the afternoon ensemble while
my body's on the sea . . .
And then: dance the Twist, breathlessly dance for Africa delivered!
The Twist—and, like once upon the Pier, the Hadaoui.
Be free men, punks.
Build an administration, construct a raceless culture.
Understand why my death is optimistic.
I'm not committing suicide. I'm living.

Here's my signature:

And I draw a sun.

Pointe Pescade, Algiers, January 23–26, 1964

II.

TO CONJURE UP THE DIRGE

1.

Comes the day when once again
                         you believe
in space, the stone
where sunlight on your eyelids is a kidskin stop.
Joy is passing 12,564 effervescent colors between your eyelashes
—There's a stupendous electricity!
Then you throw away your old underwear, your superfluous beard,
        you sing
and kids listen to you. They listen to Jean Sénac the poet.
They say: "There's a poem of the Algerian poet Jean Sénac in our
        book."
In a flash they've peopled the jasmine grating. You sing
for a bit of common clarity because the nation's on the march
in you—like marrow! You've rediscovered the gaze that beholds
what's flowing in the earth
and driving the tree.
Not necessarily tears, the gaze
                         from the source
of the bird's song on the reforested mountain,
calling to him, the worker of inner power,
the gaze from within that has meaning outside
—and keeps the land intact!
All this because a passerby has put a single phrase
        into your hand,
because his pupils fix on yours
like those punch cards

—And we know,
you know, that death has that mildew taste you despise
in damp rooms. With a cry
you wash the tiles. You shout: "Sunlight!" And your faithful sun
rises again.
Let's go to the Pier together and spell out
the line down there that defines the world: l'ho
(the water!), l'hor (the gold!), l'ho-ri-zon.
That way laughter will rebegin fresh in your belly.
L'ho (the dawn!), l'hor (not horrible, oracle!), the horizon.
There's some jump in your step now.
Let's go!

2.

Throw your death sandals into the sea!
A fish sparkles
A violet sea urchin
on the plundered sand
all the splendor.
Look, seaweed,
iron, and life
are burning in
the depths!
You fling your death sandals into the sea.
You're leaping, crazy ol' soul,
you're happy,
you're not in control,
you . . .
Yes, you're beautiful
like the Long March!

like the victory of Vietnam!
like a painting by Khadda,
      a relief by Martinez,
      Happy Arabia of Baya,
      all the colors of Zérati,
like an aquarelle by Aksouh,

               a landscape by Maisonseul,
      the Noun of Benanteur and the Alif of an owl.

3.

. . . Now that came from an opacity so far off
you don't believe your own snout! . . .

4.

Then, as one seems suspicious to them,
they stick their yellow star on the chest of my song
as they continue massacring Mayakovsky like Lorca
and throwing Nazim's audacity to the teeth of dogs,
My soul, O my twister, what's the difference now!

5.

It all began after the Night of Doubt
among the poor, the poorest in these burbs,
in this naked room, this office of the Republic of the Poor:
a blanket on the floor
               and the coffee.

It all began with a word
                              so clear
and a smile
              so clearly of
friendship
              that you didn't even feel
your marrow coming to itself on the way.
(And you were astonished on going out that your bones had
              returned
              to their place
—you felt them clear up to the blue of the sky,
all that blue you were gazing at, so blue,
the joy of the graffiti burned like a blue thistle under your skin.)

It all began with a smile from Ali.

6.

A smile as well as a castle caving in.
It sufficed for one night, mornings are bitter now
while the bus veers in the middle of the sea.

7.

A few moments
                    A few cries
The rose and the nettle.
Then a long breath.
The page that covers us at the mouth of the sea.

Let's sit on this last rock together,

we've given a first name to every hour.
Change and generosity preside at our parties.
The verb is that kid going between orders of coffee
while Amin El Hadj's playing a prelude.
There are nights for our pain
but nights for our joy as well.

I love you.

To get to you: a tunnel of brambles,
an arrogance of foam,
the dawn.
To come back: the sun
and always the tunnel of brambles.

8.

"Your chest sings in Arabic!"
Rachid, astonished, hears those independent words,
the majority of which I don't know, going into the shade.

9.

From sun to sea urchin
through a road of nerve endings
right up to the barbed wire,
your name on a stone.

Lips and spine,
sea urchin, the words,

your mouth on my skin traces the new flower
from your soul to mine, from my bones to yours,
the oxalis and the new vocabulary

                              spurt.

You're the urchin who troubles my night.

                    10.

You leave ancient vanity to the sea.
Your skin splinters. You pull pieces of glass from your veins,
one by one. You grow big, and even the jellyfish
are your afternoon comrades.

                    11.

Wicked cunning gnaws at your
blood, your guts.
Your knees buckle.

                    12.

I've drawn your lips in the sand and bitten
through to the other side.
The cosmonauts themselves have responded to my ecstasy,
but you've run away, granite before my impulses.
What's life for, then?
Why death?
And as for Revolution, why is its big gob of saliva on our tongues?

If our flesh isn't that rose that opens
beyond the portal through which April appears,
if my desire isn't a pomegranate of welcome,
if my heart is surrounded by flint and nettles,
what are these farms and factories and 500,000 trees for?
For repopulating, but what?
I bury my head in the sheets
and can't even find our silence anymore.
And what about the administration, tell me, and the kids at school
          learning my poems?
Instead, throw my verses into the fire—they've got worms
—and without even the green of hope,
and my soul's nothing more than a can of pestilence
at my window open to desert brawls.

13.

In the shift of the palm trees, in the
blue of the pool, the funereal
lamenting, the bronzed
fruity laughter offered
to the kids at the entrance,
your name rises up: fennec,
or rose of the sands!

(Or a thousand graffiti:
obscene ones, loving ones,
political ones, demented ones,
which your syllables reclaw on my nape,
your two turbulent syllables
that disable my entire blood . . .)

14.

No, don't bite my lips, sing;
my wickedness is deeper than the waters.

15.

One instant, just one, but it's important to inscribe it
on the blazons of our hearts.
We've only got time to watch over the initial letters
(those anxious frescoes, those rinds at the end
of our fingernails)
before nightfall.

16.

Beauty, fragile sister, my revolutionary!

17.

Swimmers, invade the poem with a long blue cry!
(The house has been deserted for so very long . . .)

18.

A morning that rises up in white and blue,
the interrogation of Nour, the tears of Smail
(my son at his chores and Francoise at the vegetables),

a morning weaving in and out of the room reconciling you
        to the day,
a crisp, naked, September seaside morning
(with two birds in the palm trees
and a bumblebee of a Vespa gunning away).
A completely sleek dry-water morn, all blue,
there, a life can get on.
(A little water and the geranium sits up.
A little tenderness—Nour's letter—and your pores relax.
Breathe, O soon-to-be-alert one, breathe by inventing wings for
        yourself.)

19.

Beauty, O strong sister, my revolutionary!

20.

Zerati has fetched me three snappers and medlars.
He looks at the sea. He laughs.
With a squint he denounces deception
and throws out his symbols like an assault on happiness.
Cabinet maker, mason, and cosmonaut,
such are his works.

21.

The unicorn has broken his horn, and the poem
                                is bleeding.

22.

My chest sings in Arabic.

23.

And if it's only a dream
you know it's also constructed of bricks,
but by the hands of man.

24.

If you're not beautiful like a government committee
            like the abolition of the death-pang
            like Bella Akhmadulina
            and her son in shackles
                    like the confident crowds of Diaz Ojeda,
if you're not beautiful like the Peuhle Girl in
        the Tassili Frescoes
            like the Lady of Elche
            like Aicha came came
            when the drum beats at Maithili,
if you're not beautiful like Jacques's smile
            like Jacques's guitar
            like Jacques on his tractor,
or Patrick in his Ballad
                    or Ahmed when he gives his
        flesh to the big black flame of his love,
if you're not beautiful as the day that still hesitates between daylight
        and daylight,

if you're not beautiful as a rose,

                                why live?

25.

Why die if not because a twig
suddenly lets go of the branch or that nothing
exists anymore in the forest
                      neither
                        tree
                        nor
                        sky
                        nor
                        bird
                        nor
              the unique living root?
One doesn't conjure up the Dirge.

26.

My best friend has . . . me.

27.

But I know that there still exists here men "who aren't just alloys."
I know, Nazim, but their emergence sure is slow!

28.

Your body gives itself outrageously,
it delivers me from grimaces.

29.

With a twirl of your flowery skirt, zap my rowdy street Arabs!
O come on, my sweet little tuffy,
                    beautiful as the 16 bronzes of Ife!

30.

All phrases shed to conjure up the Dirge,
what's left for you, O heart that utters roses,
what's left for you but this metamorphosis:
instead of the sting, a tree that's smitten?

You know it for such a long,
long time light and death have been irrigating you
in the same torrent.
You're walking under seaweed.
The ANISRAF train is traveling through you
(Chanterelle? Pupil? Rubbish?
Rainbow of axle grease? Mast?)
O that ferocious voice! That sun between you and yourself!

The struggle's going to be a hard one,

and you'll reach the Rose, vanquisher,

the burned bones.

Algiers, January 28, 1964
Bou Saada-El Biar, May 1965
Pointe Pescade, June 2, 1966

• 49

Words with Walt Whitman

1.

Walt Whitman, at a time when liberty's collapsing around us like an
           abandoned hotel,
and the middlemen are on the rise in every direction,
lying in wait for our last words,
give us lung and that "ardent pang of contact"
           by which our eyes have kept watch on the storm.
The furniture's sold, Walt Whitman, comrades are writhing in fear
trying just to get hold of a sprig of daylight.
It'll take a long time before our heart gets used to the noises in the
           sand,
and yet this saliva coming at us, dry and briny,
           is already the whole sea.

A sea urchin that stings will cut us loose as a clock wakes it up,
and we'll cry out: sunlight! There where the blue invades us.
O days heavy with expectation! Nights of needy breathing time!
O those kids playing ball with a flying scarab,
that supple oration of muscles in the grass,
those apricots spoiled not by axle grease but by fragrant slime,
kids black and golden as after a tournament in sepia!
Heartfelt days,
days distant and yet oh so near!
One second here at the edge of centuries
and the plunges make us dizzy as swallows.
O light! O sea! O discrete desire amid all this space!
And the high walls!
I'm singing with you, Walt Whitman,
the *camarado* you were waiting for has arrived
and already is thrusting a restlessness of rye into your beard.
"I don't wait for either sadness or approval in the words of others.
I don't consider that moonlight nostalgia.

What I look for, comrade, is the athlete in top shape
and the naked word haloed by its liquor.
What I look for, mouth to mouth,
is the sun in an uncooked word."
O Walt Whitman,
and you rebuff my thistles!
I have to get back on the road again,
traveling, traveling toward the heart of summer,
from there traveling, traveling toward the Center again,
and getting back on the road again
and traveling on
and traveling on.

2.

Comrades in the distance,
remember what it is we've suffered for,
those nights when we were subjected
to the chilling vanity
before your name exploded,
free men, good men.

Our daring was but the gropings and angers
and bitter taste of that truth that kept us upright.
The compassion of our friends
fell upon us like fruits in the wind,
they built untold citadels on our heart.
We combined with a drop of water, a point of light
—hell, with such arrogance!
(Holding on to a broken piece of the road
while having to look at desert all around!)

Then came loneliness like a never-made bed.

Where predatory claws fall
on our arms, let's imagine your kiss ever new,
that wine that doesn't lie
and makes drunkenness a beneficence.

So it's necessary to end the day
by invoking you coming through the skylight
so that children are born
and the wheat doesn't rot on the air.

Without the hope in your action,
what would we, comrades so far away, do
but moan and construct an
unfinished house of tears.

3.

And Walt Whitman, once again behind the ramparts of Spain
shaking his dove-like thighs like ashes,
enters the sea up to his shoulders
and swims,
and young men will look at him forgetting the French in bikinis for
       a moment.
And I see in the distance and to the right, stretched
between the delirious bronze, like a flock of ships,
three poets.
Federico, the first to hold a rose in his hand and a balcony shadow
       on his heart, like a logical reason,
and Miguel who's still clenching fig-tree leaves in his fist for his

friend Raymond Sitje,
and Blas, simple as a stump of wood the sea's given back.
Three poets come from common people's districts, from the fields,
each one celebrating you, Walt Whitman,
while your harmonious body is writing its cantata in big
        breaststrokes
(to Spain, to liberty,
to our night, fragile humanity).

And I've picked up a pebble and
walked it a long while on my lips
before saying the first word.

Peniscola, August 1959

Summoning the Diwan of the Pier

For Abdallah Benanteur
For Maria Manton and Louis Nallard

TOWARD A SUN

I sing man in transition
busted at heart, garish
with wounds.
I challenge the dread that's struck us at the core,
the poisoned word that's put our mouth under its spell.
I exist in my negation
going forward toward a bit of water.

O People!
Revolution!
I sing, to our puddles of man uprooted,
superb health,
the sun seen full-face.
I sing for the living
hand
in my hand.
It's then the words of the poet are clear. . . .

Paris, 1960

Punks, respect the body,
love it right into distress.
The muscle hardening at the stroke
is the soul suddenly broken like bread and shared,
is the spouse glorifying you with her desire,
the sunlight on motionless stone.

O punks, beauty submitted as evidence!

Through the nubile branches
of this March afternoon,
I've recognized you, athletes!
Bread! Fountainhead! Sacrament!
And I've cried out amid the iron
(swearing an oath on my future race):
sun young and precise as their movements.

Paris, 1959

Brahim, the Generous

For Brahim Djaballah

1.

You've given light and peace back to me,
the curve in the abrupt upgrade,
the science of shafts and the modesty of water.
The new tongue breaks through my teeth
like the first reed in a rock.
The steppe's already smiling,
the trees are en route.
You've also made this withered heart your Domain.

2.

I'm flooded with nobility,
the fig tree spills its gaze.
Citizen of the desert,
it's enough that you simply move;
I've never seen the sea so blue.

3.

You command my gaze,
pull my senses out of chaos,
you break in with dignity
and tender reason.
And if the white, the blue-green make such a eulogy,
it's because the ochre
has stirred the water down there.

4.

Djaballah! God's given him to me!
Caught in a snag, one makes up a phrase,
the dissolute soul roars and its head demolishes
walls.
And suddenly effortlessly the question shifts
from interrogation to the bashful place
where the joyless heart
answers that the invasion is good and that
the rain hasn't come in vain.
God's given him to me. The blocked
poem's on the high road again.
—But how tough the climb for this crazy leg!

5.

Never has the Amiraute dock been so beautiful;
it's because the first derring-do has blossomed in the desert.

6.

I'm alone.
But never has the thistle known a more fertile land.
Your look irrigates the space
where I drink.
Never as well have I been so peopled by chance:
the happiness of building a mirage with you.

7.

I sing you.
The sea and the steppe.
I sing.
Who have found those happy lips
where the word looks beautiful!

Bou Saada, April 12–13, 1966
Pointe Pescade, April 15, 1966

An Island against Death

These words that escape with all their teeth
under our kisses, the whole sea
on your chest drawing me
toward the blues, the red, the mornings
sprayed in blond down,
those dreams flooded by saliva,
those odysseys and Diwans,
those arms like a vocabulary
for crossing out rhymes as insulting,
all those sails: your caresses,
my blazings up. My shyness,
tell me, O my love, is the horror over?
Is death breaking its fronds?
Has the poem been delivered
for a century? For a single instant?

(Dense and downright as thighs
are the words that never will turn yellow.)

Pointe Pescade, June 13, 1966